Thunder Bay Press
An imprint of the Advantage Publishers Group
THUNDER BAY   5880 Oberlin Drive, San Diego, CA 92121-4794
P · R · E · S · S   www.thunderbaybooks.com

Produced by PRC Publishing,
an imprint of the Anova Books Company Ltd,
151 Freston Road, London W10 6TH, U.K.

ISBN-13: 978-1-59223-405-9
ISBN-10: 1-59223-405-4

Library of Congress Cataloging-in-Publication Data

Brown, Christopher, 1954–
   Sign language for babies and toddlers / by Christopher Brown and John Clements;
illustrations by Anne-Marie Sonneveld.
      p. cm.
   Includes index.
   ISBN-13: 978-1-59223-405-9
   ISBN-10: 1-59223-405-4
   1. Nonverbal communication in infants. 2. Interpersonal communication in infants. 3.
Nonverbal communication in children. 4. Interpersonal communication in children. 5.
Child rearing. 6 Sign language. I. Clements, John (John Bernard) II. Title.

BF720.C65B76 2005
419'.7'0832—dc22

                                                                                    2005050651

Printed and bound in China

2 3 4 5 09 08 07 06

Contents

Introduction

Since the beginning of human civilization, we have had a basic need to communicate with others. But before speech evolved, how did we achieve this? It is likely that a very basic version of sign language evolved, a series of signals to represent primal needs: food, water, and, most importantly, danger.

Sign language is an important part of the evolution of language. Left to our own devices, when we find ourselves in a situation where spoken language is inappropriate, it is our natural reaction to revert to some form of sign language. Someone who is not familiar with sign language, a hearing person for example, may only use it in its most basic form. This may be a slightly less exact method of communication, but it is one that transcends the boundaries of the spoken word. For this reason, it is also something that can be used by children before they know how to speak, as the desire to communicate is a primal instinct. It is quite natural for babies and toddlers, whose speech has not yet developed, to use this communication tool.

We have all experienced frustration at not being able to communicate an important message to someone who does not speak our language and where basic, improvised sign language will not suffice. It is this kind of frustration that children experience when they are trying to relate their wants and needs to parents and other adults. Their brains have developed to the point where these wants and needs are evident to them, but their speech has not yet developed, making such communication difficult. However, the use of basic sign language can help young children in this situation. The purpose of this book is to try to give you an insight into this important and exciting field.

You are probably wondering what baby signs are, and whether or not they come from an actual sign language. If it were possible to use ASL (American Sign Language), then that would probably be the obvious answer. Sadly, life is not that simple! American Sign Language is a method of signed communication used by adults and older children—in other words, by people who have reached their full development in terms of manual dexterity. It would be great if very young children could be taught to use as many of the ASL signs as possible. They would then have a basic knowledge of ASL, which would enable them to communicate with people who do not hear well, especially as children with hearing difficulties are now being educated in mainstream schools. However, young children are not able to form all the necessary ASL hand shapes. Another reason as to why it is best to be inventive when teaching a baby or toddler to sign is that learning at this age should always be fun. Learning any form of sign language should become a delightful game between a baby and his or her parents.

A baby's mind is a blank canvas with none of the preconceived ideas that society imposes upon us as we develop: For example, the ASL sign for "dog" involves the middle finger and thumb being snapped at waist level, as if calling a dog to

come. This is something that an adult with absolutely no knowledge of formal sign language would probably instantly recognize for what it is meant to signify—the sign is a mime of an action that would be familiar to most people. A baby, however, would not be familiar with it and might see the dog as something with a soft and silky coat that he or she enjoys patting gently. If you and your baby are mutually happy to use this gentle patting motion while raising and lowering your hand, then you should adopt this as your sign for "dog" because that is how your baby recognizes it within his or her own realm of perception.

The most important thing to remember is that sign language at this level is not meant to do anything more than to enable families to communicate with their youngest members. Just as most families have the odd special word to describe an object—perhaps a word that they made up and whose origin is shrouded in an unusual event—so, too, should your own family's sign language evolve using the signs that are the most effective for everyone, especially the youngest members. Using some formal signs based on American Sign Language would be very useful in the long term, but they are not mandatory in establishing a communication system with the newest member of the family.

There has been a great deal of recent debate regarding the developmental implications of teaching sign language to young children who have not yet begun to speak. Some argue that a functional communication skill through sign language might seriously delay the child using his or her verbal skills. This has not proven to be the case. Early development of communication in this way has actually been shown to expedite vocal skills once speech has begun.

Imagine a scenario where you are trying to buy something in a foreign country, but you and the seller do not speak the same language. Neither

party would just give up on the situation, but would instead perhaps develop a form of sign language to communicate. Just as trying to establish sign language communication with the seller in a foreign marketplace would be taken in small steps and by using trial and error, the same thing would be experienced with your baby. However, using trial and error, until the message had been adequately expressed, would make the experience rather lengthy and drawn out. Imagine introducing a translator into the situation, someone who is fluent in both languages and able to drastically reduce the time involved in such a communication. The translator would be able to remove the frustration of trying to sign one's meaning and being misunderstood several times before the true meaning is conveyed. If you were in that situation, would you tell the translator that he was not required? Of course not—you would choose the easiest, fastest, and most accurate method of being understood. Something similar applies to the baby using sign language. Once he or she realizes that speech is a faster and more accurate method of communication, then that is the method that the child will choose to use.

Early sign language skills have actually been proven to increase the speed at which a young child acquires his or her verbal skills, but why, you may wonder, does one thing precipitate the other? When using sign language with a baby, the word that the sign represents should always be verbalized as well, just as the word is always mouthed when using formal ASL. The reason that this is done with ASL is that true understanding of sign language is achieved for the hearing-impaired person in three ways. The first is by "reading" the sign that is being offered, the second is by observing the word being mouthed by the signer, and the third is by observing the body language of the signer. When using sign language with a baby, similar signals apply. When a baby is just spoken to, he cannot reply, so the parent speaking to the child has very little idea as to whether the child has really understood what has been said. Since the child is unable to reply, he cannot confirm his understanding or use the words he has been taught in a phrase to confirm that understanding has taken place. When the baby is spoken to and sign language is used simultaneously, however, understanding is frequently confirmed, as the baby is able to repeat the sign back to the parent or to use it in another context.

In this way, the baby's vocabulary list has already started to form. The parents can know that their child has understood words before speech is possible, and they are then able to progress and gradually introduce more vocabulary. The end result of this is that once the child is able to verbalize, he or she has already acquired a great deal of vocabulary. The child's vocabulary is then much wider than that of a child who was not taught signing at a very young age. With this wider vocabulary in place, the child does not have to learn the meaning of these words as well as how to speak them, but instead learns how to pronounce words he already knows while learning more.

Apart from the joy of being able to communicate with your child at a much earlier age than if you had to wait for spoken communication to begin, there are many other advantages. The most obvious one is the way that it enables many potential frustrating situations—for both babies and parents—to be resolved. Just imagine not being able to tell someone that you were hungry or thirsty, that you had injured yourself, or that you were uncomfortable or even just plain fed up. This is the frustration that babies often endure. The way they express their frustration is, of course, in typical baby fashion, with which every parent will be familiar. Similarly for parents, having a discontented and frustrated baby is a far from pleasant experience. Sign language can ease this situation greatly. Perhaps if all parents used this communication tool with babies, it's possible that the "terrible twos" could become an old myth. Parents naturally have a strong bond with their children; however, by enabling communication before speech it is possible to actually enhance this bond, since the baby and his or her parents are able to interact without guesswork being involved.

About Baby Signing

Sign language for babies is not a new invention. Until now, the majority of parents with hearing children have not even considered the idea of using sign language to communicate with their babies. They have been content knowing that, with the natural development of their baby into childhood, she will acquire verbal skills that will enable her to communicate. However, even these parents will at some point have encouraged their baby to wave good-bye and to make a few other basic signs that are recognized throughout the hearing adult world—signs that are universal and easily identified by all. We are familiar with how babies, for example, stretch their arms forward when they want human contact. The idea is to extend the visual language that the baby is already trying to achieve for herself and establish a nonverbal communication system to enable her needs to be identified and catered to by her parents. The baby's own willingness to communicate is already evident at this stage—we are simply enabling the infant to build on her inherent desire.

The formalized use of sign language with infants has been around for over forty years, but probably the greatest exponent of this communication tool is Dr. Joseph Garcia. He began to appreciate the potential of signing with babies after observing deaf parents communicating with their children. He noticed that they were able to communicate with their children in sign language at a much earlier age than hearing parents were able to begin the verbal communication process. He then began studying this in detail, using his own sons as examples by teaching them sign language as soon as they were able to absorb the skill prior to speech, and then monitoring their use of it and their progress in acquiring verbal skills.

The system of sign language that Dr. Garcia used to communicate with children was American Sign Language, which was developed in North America by Thomas Hopkins Gallaudet, an American who studied the methods for teaching deaf students in France and then returned to America to found a school for the deaf in Hartford, Connecticut. As with all languages, spoken and signed, ASL is a living language that constantly evolves and changes. This has brought us to where ASL is today. In order to meet the needs of an extensive

contemporary vocabulary, hand shapes have to be used that may sometimes take a little practicing to achieve, since the majority of us are not used to having to manipulate our fingers into these complex positions. In fact, one of the downfalls for an elderly deaf person who signs can be the onset of arthritis in the hands, making the formation of certain signs difficult. Until a child's hands are fully developed, he or she too will find it difficult to make many of the recognized signs, which is another reason for developing some unique signs for use between the parent and child. The sign language currently being used for babies and toddlers, however, is loosely based on formalized American Sign Language signs, and there are several advantages to using this method. The most important thing to remember is that there is a large deaf and hearing-

impaired community, and the more people who have a knowledge of sign language, the more people they are easily able to communicate with and the more they are able to fully participate in the hearing world. One never knows when one will need to communicate with someone in sign language, and acquiring this skill at an early age is a tremendous advantage.

As discussed in the introduction to this book, the major advantage of using sign language at this early stage in your child's development is to alleviate all the frustrations of being unable to communicate. If you imagine yourself suddenly being unable to speak, then you may begin to realize the magnitude of the problems you could face. As an infant, the problems would, of course, not be so great, but nevertheless they would be frustrating and uncomfortable. However, there are many other valid reasons for why such use of sign language is a distinct advantage. Apart from the obvious benefits, in terms of preparing for spoken communication, there are other issues in favor of using sign language with children at a young age.

The bond between the infant and parent is an important one. It is good to make the child feel loved and protected by her parents during this important developmental stage. Once sign language communication has become possible, this bond is strengthened in many ways and at a much earlier stage than it is with a child who has not acquired verbal skills. To begin with, communication removes the guesswork involved in figuring out what is wrong with an unhappy child. The parent is able to deal with whatever problem presents itself in terms of the child's needs, and the child realizes at a very early age that this interaction with her parents is present and that these are the nurturing people who are truly dealing with her desires. A child that is trying to find someone to understand her will often gravitate from one person to another until someone hits on the idea as to what it is the child truly wants.

In terms of dealing with the level of communication that has been established, this too strengthens the bond between parents and children, since they are able to share much more at an earlier stage in their relationship. We, as our parents' children and some as parents of children, will have all shared the joys of storytelling at an early age. Prior to speech, children are only able to listen to the story and parents are only able to tell the story. However, when sign language is involved in the scenario, such storytelling at an early age becomes an interactive experience for all, something to be shared and something that can bring us closer together. As parents, when we read a story, apart from speaking the words, we are able to make the relevant signs and encourage children to copy the signs with us, perhaps repeating each sign after we have made it, then repeating the entire phrase and signing it together. This is so rewarding for both the child and parents. Of course, one must always remember that any kind of learning is much easier when accompanied by a huge dose of fun. When this is included, learning becomes an enjoyable event and something that is looked forward to and consequently used and practiced as often as possible.

How to Start

Every child is an individual and develops at his or her own rate. Parents of more than one child will agree that perhaps one of their children has walked at a very early age, whereas another has not acquired the skill quite so early, but has surprised them by becoming potty trained on practically the first attempt. So it is with learning sign language: there is no hard-and-fast rule that can be applied. It is simply a matter of watching and waiting until the child indicates that he or she is ready to begin to communicate.

This stage will gradually become evident as your child starts to indicate that he wishes to start communicating. You will notice that he has an increased awareness of his surroundings and is looking for responses; for example, he may begin to wave good-bye or point at objects. As parents, you will know when it is time for your baby to start getting familiar with some basic signs. It is said that this should usually occur between nine and twelve months of age, but as we have already discussed, no rule applies to every child in terms of development, so do not be afraid to try earlier or later, whenever you as the parent feel it is appropriate. Incidentally, there will be no harm done should you decide to sign as you speak to your baby soon after birth.

Once you have begun to sign, do not expect your baby to immediately reply in the same way. It is a gradual process, but with patience, your dedication will be rewarded. Remember when you learned your first foreign language at school? Once you understood the meaning of a word or phrase, it took a while before you acquired the confidence to use it yourself. However, having no inhibitions, babies will respond quickly and willingly once the connection from brain to hand has been established. In fact, sometimes they will sign so quickly that we may miss what they are trying to tell us, so be sure to watch closely!

In terms of looking for a response, you may well find that the first indication of understanding from a child is that he or she is continually repeating the same sign and obviously applying it to many different objects. If this does happen, do not be disheartened or discouraged—consider it to be an indicator that contact has been made and the brain is responding in conjunction with the hands. To look at this another way, if you think about a child who has no sign language but is learning to speak in the conventional manner, very often the same thing happens, sometimes at the most embarrassing times! After all, we all have favorite family stories of how some important guests have come to meet a baby and he smiled profusely and delighted everyone and then pointed to the delivery man, giggled, and cooed "Dada." Well, it's exactly the same idea at work here: the communication channel has opened, and it is just a question of patiently coaching him and reinforcing his knowledge as to the meaning of that particular sign. Understanding will come with patience and encouragement.

In the previous chapter, it was mentioned that some of the signs used in ASL are quite difficult to form. This actually applies to an adult who has not signed before, since one does not usually need this amount of manual dexterity for everyday purposes. For someone with arthritis or for a child who is still physically developing, this makes forming certain signs particularly difficult. A simple example of this would be the ASL sign for the letter R, which involves crossing the middle finger over the index finger. Although in an ideal world every child would learn to sign using ASL and thus be able to communicate with all hearing-impaired people, this is just not a practical option, although ASL can be used as a solid base and starting point.

Apart from the manual dexterity issue, there is another reason why other signs can and should be used. When trying to teach a baby or toddler to sign, we are dealing with a mind that has not yet gained any preconceived ideas and, in its virgin creative state, may well see and feel things in a different way than an adult does. It will be much easier for a child to remember and learn a sign that he has invented to represent a particular object in the way that the child perceives it himself, rather than trying to impose a sign for him to learn. For example, the sign for "horse" is two fingers placed at the right temple, moved up and down twice. If you imagine what this represents to an adult, the sign will conjure up the image of a horse's long and pointed ear. However, to a child, that may well not be an image that easily comes to mind, despite the fact that he would be able to form the correct hand shape. But when that child is taken to feed the horses, he enjoys the way the horse leans across the fence to get its treat. In that child's mind, he sees the horse gently bowing his head down. Communicating the word "horse" to him will become represented by a gentle bowing of the arm back and forth. You will actually find that this becomes not only great fun, but a tremendous insight into the child's mind by revealing how a child perceives certain things that with knowledge and education an adult has come to perceive in a rather different way.

Anyone who has had any formal training as a teacher will endorse the fact that one of the most important tools for good teaching is to work within a framework—to have a lesson plan and to record what has been achieved and when. This philosophy is also important when teaching your baby to sign. The lesson plan, of course, does not apply, but for purposes of continuity and being able to really assimilate what has been learned, it is highly advisable for the parent to keep an accurate diary of events. It is most useful to record what has been taught right from the very first attempt and to note when you have confirmation that the sign has been understood by means of your child using it back to you. This will form the basis of many lists of vocabulary. While learning new words, it is, of course, important to ensure that the old ones are used frequently, so as not to be forgotten.

Before starting any attempt to sign, remember that anyone will learn more easily if they are enjoying what they are doing and having fun with a purpose. You must always be sure to make your child's learning an enjoyable and fun-filled experience, something she associates with play and pleasure. Ideally, set aside some quality time every day, preferably at the same time so that the learning routine is established early. Make sure that you have no interruptions, as you need to give your child your undivided attention during this period. The more pleasurable you are able to make this experience, the faster she will learn and the more fulfilling it will become for both of you on many levels.

You may wonder which would be the first signs to try to teach your child. We are all familiar with parents' attempts to get their children to say "Mommy" and "Daddy." However, a baby's inherent needs are more along the lines of comfort. In other words, initially addressing hunger and thirst are of primal importance. Another consideration when beginning this journey into communication is that it helps if the first signs are very easy to form. With these two ideas in mind, the time has come to begin.

When you are ready to introduce the first signs to your child, bear in mind that this is something that will require dedication, patience, and a great deal of persistence before the reward of receiving sign language back from your child is reaped. Since children have only a short attention span, do not try to confuse your child with more than one or two signs to begin with. You need to constantly repeat the sign while speaking the word it represents and using animated voice inflection and positive body language to endorse the meaning of the word. Of course, you need to be sure when doing this that you have your baby's full attention, and you need to repeat the sign in this manner frequently. Obviously, it then becomes a redundant exercise if your little one's attention is wandering because of the antics of siblings, a dog's barking, or a loud television. Ensure that your delivery of the sign and its spoken word is as effervescent as possible, but more importantly, be sure that you closely observe that the sign is being received by its intended recipient.

Another thing that is worth mentioning here is that we have previously discussed the fact of trying to use as many ASL-based signs as possible, but that on occasion many unique signs will be invented and become an integral part of the vocabulary used between parent and child. If you were not interested in communication with your child using sign language, you would not be reading this book. Regardless of how keen and enthusiastic you may be about this subject, it is a redundant exercise for you to learn a vast list of ASL vocabulary in advance. Just as every child is different, so too will be the specific vocabulary used by that child in terms of which ASL-based signs are used and which are invented. If you should take the time to acquire a huge ASL vocabulary, you may then become confused yourself, should you and your child invent a unique sign for a word you have already learned through ASL. It is much better, therefore, for you both to learn new signs at the same time and avoid any confusion.

Before we suggest some basic words that may be useful for you to begin with, let us just touch upon what sort of response you should be looking for in terms of your child's comprehension. Because the sign is always being taught in conjunction with a spoken word, an encouraging indication that things are starting to gel in your child's mind is when a familiar word is spoken and the infant starts to look for the sign to be made that corresponds to that particular word. This initial understanding may well be built upon your noticing that your child has suddenly seemed to understand what you are referring to, even if he has not yet been able to return the sign. For example, if you have been teaching the word "dog" and your pet suddenly happens to wander up when you are signing this word and your child then points to the dog, this is an indicator that understanding has taken place.

The truly big momentous occasion will, of course, be when your child starts to sign back to you. As we have touched upon earlier, do not worry if the same sign is applied to everything or if a sign that has been learned and used for a while suddenly seems to have been forgotten. At this early stage in his or her life, your child is undergoing many changes in terms of growth and development, so it is not surprising that there are times when he or she may become confused or appear to forget. Apart from making it a great deal of fun, the true key to teaching sign language at this early age is constant use and repetition, and by using this method you will be amazed by the results you and your child are able to achieve.

Number, Shapes, the Alphabet, and Movements

Our first section is more of a visual guide to commonly used hand shapes, rather than a vocabulary list. It is our intention that your understanding of the illustrations will be clear enough for you to accurately be able to make the signs shown. However, without being able to show a three-dimensional moving image, there are occasions when it is imperative to understand the written description of making the sign in order to be able to interpret it accurately. To avoid very lengthy and repetitive descriptions, expressions like "inverted 2 hand" and "C hand" are often used when explaining signs. (This is also the case with many American Sign Language dictionaries.) This section is intended to remove the frustration from trying to interpret such descriptions. Apart from possibly being used to teach your child how to count in sign language, this section should be used purely as a key to the subsequent sections.

1

2

3

4

5

6

7

8

9

10

A

B

C

D

E

F

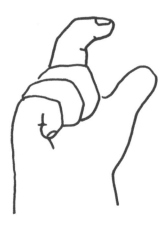

G

H

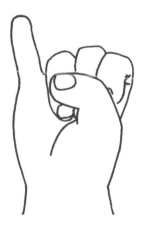

K

L

M

N

O

P

Q

R

S

T

U

V

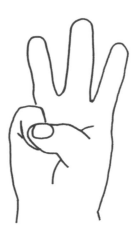

W

X

Sign Language for Babies and Toddlers

Y

Z

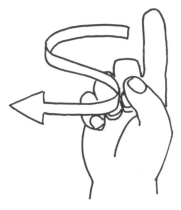

These hand shapes are shown for reference purposes only, to be used as a guide when forming a hand shape based on a letter or number.

INVERTED 2 HAND

BENT 2 HAND

BENT 5 HAND

MODIFIED 8 HAND

Sign Language for Babies and Toddlers

FLAT O HAND

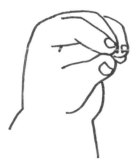

CUPPED HAND

CLAW HAND

SINGLE MOVEMENT

DOUBLE MOVEMENT

Twenty ASL Signs to Begin

These twenty basic ASL signs are a good place to start the learning process. When reading the written descriptions of how to form these signs for basic hand shapes and numbers, please refer to the previous section.

Looking at these signs from the point of view of an adult, you can easily understand the thought process as to how these particular signs were formed. Your child, without an adult's experience, may well be unable to associate the significance of some of these signs with his own limited experience. This is the time when a unique sign, significant to him and understood by you, may well prove to be more effective and much easier to learn because he will be able to relate to its significance. You do not need to rigidly follow the signs that are given here, and may find it more effective to adapt your own.

Let's discuss a couple of examples, such as the sign for the word "cookie." We understand the significance of the cookie cutter; an older child may well have helped his mother with the baking. However, a baby or toddler would be kept away from anything sharp and usually has a much lower field of vision, so he may well have never seen this process taking place. But imagine forming a ring with the thumb and index finger (as if holding the outside of a small cookie) and moving the hand toward the mouth—this is something that would be within a child's realm of experience and a much more relevant and memorable sign for you to use. Another good example is the sign for "big." The sign shown here does not instantly convey the meaning that it is meant to portray unless a dose of adult-sized imagination is thrown into the equation. However, by modifying it slightly, it instantly conveys its intended meaning. So picture standing with palms together in front of the chest and moving them out and away from each other. (Puffing out the cheeks would help to create the requisite image.) Again, this now becomes something that is instantly recognizable, more of a pantomime sign than an ASL one, but something that a child can more easily relate to.

Don't forget that creating new signs can be fun and interesting on a variety of levels and, strangely, just as we tend never to forget the words that children invented, mispronounced, or used in an incorrect context, similarly, the signs that will be best remembered and probably retained for an entire lifetime are those that were the fun invention of a child's active mind and the manifestation of his own perception as to how things appeared to be.

By using a group of about twenty words as your initial foundation, try to make sure that these words are understood and your child is able to use them in the appropriate context before attempting anything further. Don't forget, time is on your side. If this process takes weeks or months, don't get frustrated—just allow your child to learn at his own pace and only then begin to increase his vocabulary.

MOMMY

R "5" hand, palm L, fingertips up, tap chin with thumb twice.

DADDY

R "5" hand, palm L, tap forehead with thumb twice.

PLEASE

Rub R palm clockwise against chest.

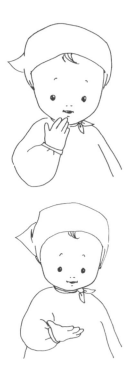

THANK YOU

Touch R hand to lips, move hand away from face.

YES

"S" hand, shake up and down.

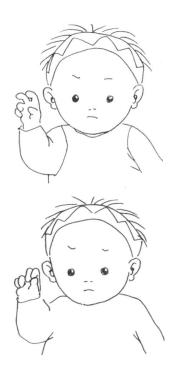

NO

Bring R index finger, middle finger, and thumb together quickly.

EAT

Place tips of R flat "O" hand on lips and replace several times.

DINNER

Move fingertips of R flat "O" hand to mouth, then place R curved
hand over flat L hand, palm down (signs "eat" and "night").

DRINK

Bring R "C" hand to mouth as if holding a glass.

MILK

Open and close hands to mime milking a cow.

COOKIE

Place fingertips of R "C" hand on L palm and twist
as if using a cookie cutter.

YOU

Point R index finger at other person.

HOT

Place tips of R "5" hand with fingers bent onto the
mouth and twist hand down.

HURT

Point L and R index fingers at place where pain is felt.

HELP

L "A" hand, palm R, place in R palm and raise R palm up.

Sign Language for Babies and Toddlers

BIG

Index fingers and thumbs up, move hands apart.

BALL

Place tips of hands together, outlining the shape of a ball.

GENTLE/PET

Stroking motion along back of opposite hand.

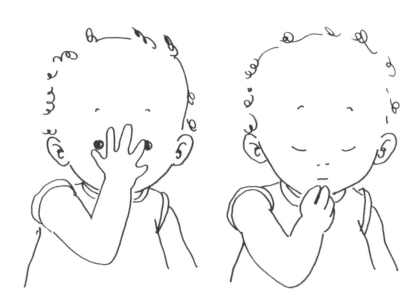

SLEEP

R "5" hand on face, palm in. Slide down,
ending with fingers together.

BYE-BYE

Wave good-bye.

Visual Vocabulary

The intention of this section is to give you a reasonably broad basis of signs that may be useful when beginning to sign to your child. The signs illustrated are all based on American Sign Language, but as we have discussed, it is entirely acceptable for you to adapt these signs or, indeed, for you to create your own signs to represent any of the words listed.

The vocabulary illustrated within this chapter has been broken down into sections, with the hope that this will make it more user-friendly, so that you will not have to struggle through many pages of an index to find a sign that you may wish to refer to quickly. It is also hoped that, by using these sections, we can give you ideas as to when and where it may be appropriate to introduce new signs and which new signs could be useful to incorporate into your growing sign language vocabulary.

The golden rule when using words from any of these sections is that no matter how many of these words are taught and understood, the only way to keep them in the active vocabulary is to use them constantly. This is where the opportunities to sign are basically up to your own inventiveness and initiative in terms of creating appropriate times for signs to be practiced. The mealtime section is perhaps a good place to start, since your child is likely to be a captive audience in the chair where she sits to eat. Before you even offer her anything to eat or drink, you can ask her if she's hungry or thirsty, then perhaps offer her a choice—does she want a banana or an apple?—and of course immediately rewarding her with the item she has asked for. Another technique used by many parents is to perhaps cut down on the amount of food given to a child, giving one the opportunity to ask if a child would like more to drink or another cookie, for example.

The nature section can be used productively in two different ways. The obvious one is to use words as you are out and about. However, the vocabulary used within that section is also applicable to many books, which are full of animals and outdoor scenes. In fact, having already stated that reading and signing texts from books is a useful learning tool, they are also a great way to reinforce the learning that has been achieved during other times. So, for example, if you have been to the park during the daytime and used words like "dog," "fish," and "horse," try to find a picture book with these things in it to use as part of your bedtime story. You will be amazed at how much you are able to practice what you have learned during the day with a little inventiveness while reading at bedtime. Once you have identified and used a certain sign, you can reinforce the lesson by referring back to when you saw that object earlier in the day. For example, if you saw a dog in the park, once you have found the dog in the book, you can then say, "We saw a dog. Was it a big dog or a small dog?"

With practice, you will become an expert at using the words learned in this way, which allows them to be repeated frequently but in an enjoyable manner and without it feeling like a formal lesson is taking place. You also need to encourage your child to talk to you, which you will find is a great deal easier once she has acquired a certain amount of formal sign language vocabulary. It is then that she will gain the confidence to be able to impart important information back to you, such as where she hurts, how she feels, or letting you know that she has an uncomfortable dirty diaper.

1.   Playtime

We have decided to nominate this category as our first section where true vocabulary is listed. Having frequently stressed the importance of combining fun with learning, playtime seems a natural place to begin. There is no hard-and-fast rule as to how to incorporate sign language instruction into playtime. Everyone will develop their own methods that work best for them. However, as a place to start, try using various brightly colored stuffed animals, as your child can learn about the type of animal, the color, and the soft feel of the toy. Remember, a young child relies heavily on her sense of touch, and the more interesting the feel of something, the more her curiosity will be aroused. Just as soft toys and stuffed animals can be used as teaching aids at playtime, bath time can be just as fun, with the use of bath toys and colored soaps and lotions.

DANCE

L hand palm up, tips out. Sweep R inverted "2" hand over palm
several times.

LISTEN

Place R cupped hand behind R ear.

LOOK

Point at eyes with R "2" hand, twist and point forward.

BOOK

Palms together, thumbs up. Open as if opening a book.

TOY

R and L "T" hands, swing in and out twice.

NOISE

Place R cupped hand behind R ear.

PLAY

Hold R and L "Y" hands in front of body and shake back and forth several times.

BICYCLE

R and L "S" hands, make pedaling motion.

SHARE

L palm facing R, brush R palm back and forth across L index finger
at 90-degree angle.

MUSIC

Move R hand back and forth over L arm, which is held in front of chest with L palm up.

BALLOON

Place R and L "S" hands at mouth, L in front of R. Move apart
while opening palms, as if forming a large balloon.

BLUE

R "B" hand, shake back and forth.

BLACK

Outline R eyebrow with R index finger.

GREEN

R "G" hand, shake back and forth.

RED

Brush lower lip with tip of R index finger and repeat.

WHITE

R "5" hand against chest, palm in, tips L. Place R fingertips on
chest and draw out into "O" sign.

ORANGE

R "C" hand, palm and fingertips L. Place at mouth,
squeeze into an "S," and repeat.

YELLOW

R "Y" hand, shake in and out.

PINK

Move middle finger of R "P" hand down across lips.

BROWN

R "B" hand against R cheek, palm out. Move down.

2.   Mealtime

It is important to establish a learning routine and set aside a regular time every day for a study session. Mealtime is an excellent opportunity to practice what has been learned because it is a frequent and regular occurrence in the daily routine. Of course, hunger and thirst are basic emotions and can be used as tools through which your child communicates his needs. It is worthwhile to offer him choices and encourage him to indicate his preferences by using sign language. Similarly, if he would like more to eat or is already satisfied, he can extend his sign language vocabulary.

MOUTH

Outline mouth with R index finger.

STOMACH

Pat stomach with R hand.

WANT

R and L claw hands in front of body, palms up. Draw both hands in toward chest.

MORE

R and L "O" hands, palms and tips facing.
Tap fingertips together twice.

THIRSTY

Draw R index finger down throat.

BANANA

Hold up L index finger, mime peeling a banana with
tips of R flat "O" hand.

APPLE

Place knuckles of R "X" hand on R cheek and twist forward.

WATER

Tap side of mouth with "W" hand.

ALL GONE

Sweep hands from center out.

CHEESE

Twist palms together.

FINISHED

Both hands in front of body, palms up. Turn both hands over.

ICE CREAM

R "S" hand in front of mouth, mime eating an ice-cream cone.

SPOON

Curved R "H" hand, place on curved L palm and move up to mouth a few times.

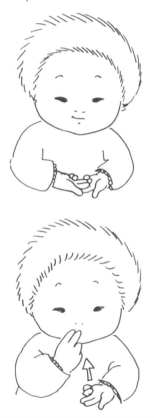

FORK

L hand palm up, tips R. Tap L palm with tips
of R inverted "2" hand.

CUP

Place R "C" hand on upturned L palm.

Sign Language for Babies and Toddlers

FULL

R hand, palm down, place against chest and move up to chin.

BOTTLE

Place R "C" hand on L palm. Lift up into an "S."

BOWL

Hold R and L cupped hands together, palms up. Move apart and
up, outlining the shape of a bowl.

PEAR

L flat "O" hand, palm in, tips R. Stroke L tips with R fingers,
ending in a R flat "O" hand.

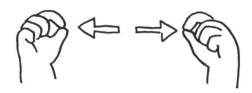

SAUSAGE

R and L "G" hands, index fingers touching. Draw apart while
opening and closing fingers, indicating links of sausage.

3. Nature

Our previous sections have all been related to indoor activities and it will be fun to vary the routine by doing some learning about the world outside. All children are stimulated by the sounds, smells, and colors of nature, and having shown interest in something outside, you can share in the enjoyment by trying to describe the event in sign language.

BEAR

Cross wrists of clawed hands and scratch upper chest.

BIRD

R "G" hand, tips forward. Place on chin and bring index finger
and thumb together twice.

CAT

Place R "F" hand on side of mouth and pull away twice.

COW

Place thumb of R "Y" hand on R temple, then twist forward.

CHICKEN

Place side of R "G" hand on mouth, then place tips in L palm.

MONKEY

Scratch sides of the body with both hands, imitating a
monkey scratching.

PIG

Place back of R hand under chin and flap tips down twice.

BEE/BUG

Place thumb on nose, wiggle index and middle fingers.

BUTTERFLY

Link thumbs and flutter fingers.

DOG

Hold hands in front like a dog begging.

ELEPHANT

From nose, trace elephant's winding trunk with "C" hand.

FLOWER

R flat "O" hand, touch both sides of nose.

HORSE

Touch thumb to side of head, flap index and
middle fingers up and down.

FISH

R palm facing L, move away from body with wiggling motion.

MOUSE

Strike tip of nose twice with R index finger.

SPIDER

Cross R and L claw hands, move forward while wiggling fingers.

Sign Language for Babies and Toddlers

TIGER

R and L claw hands at face, palms in. Pull hands away from
face, outlining tiger stripes.

TREE

R "5" hand, palm L. Place R elbow on back of L hand and
shake R hand back and forth.

CROCODILE

Open and close R and L "5" hands like jaws.

DUCK

"H" hand at mouth, palm down. Open and close index and middle fingers onto thumb.

4.   Friends and Family

It is important that your child has as much exposure to sign language as possible, and the more that family members and people who have regular contact with her are able to participate, the better. When a group of visitors is around, identifying who's who can be a fun game.

ME

Touch chest with R index finger.

WE

Touch R index finger on R side of chest and arc across to L side of chest.

BABY

Cradle arms at waist level and rock back and forth.

BOY

Snap R flat "O" hand at forehead as though touching brim of hat.

BROTHER

Snap R flat "O" sign at forehead, then tap R and L index fingers together, palms down and tips out.

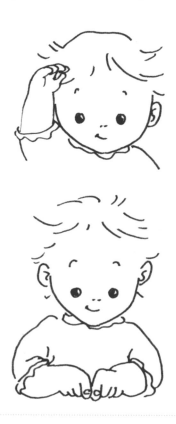

CHILD

Lower R hand, palm down, as if indicating a small child.

CHILDREN

Lower R hand, palm down, as if indicating a small child, then bounce to the R to signify more than one.

GIRL

R "A" hand, palm L, thumb on R cheek, move down jawline.

SISTER

R "A" hand, thumb on R cheek, move down jawline and then tap
R and L index fingers together, palms down and tips out.

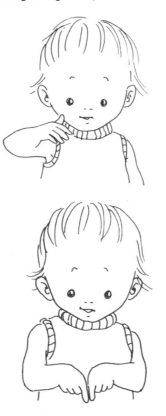

FRIEND

Cross index fingers of R and L "X" hands, then switch
position of hands and cross again.

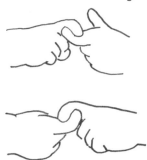

GRANDMOTHER

R "5" hand, palm L, thumb touching chin, move away in two arcs.

GRANDFATHER

R "5" hand, palm L, thumb touching forehead,
move away in two arcs.

MY

R palm flat on chest.

5.   Bedtime

Just as mealtime is a regular event at a set time, so is bedtime, another excellent opportunity to practice some signs and a time when a different vocabulary is obviously appropriate. This can, of course, be extended into the world of bedtime stories, something that most children thoroughly enjoy and look forward to. The bedtime story is something that a skillful parent can invent to incorporate many of the signs that have been used during the daytime, with specific emphasis on new words that you have been trying to teach.

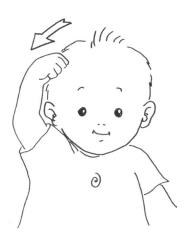

BRUSH HAIR

R "A" hand at top of head, move down side of head
twice with brushing motion.

WAKE UP

Hold index finger and thumbs of both hands over eyes, knuckles
facing each other, and open into "L" hands.

WASH

L hand palm up, tips out, rub knuckles of R "A" hand
on upturned L palm.

BED

Tilt head slightly with R palm on R cheek.

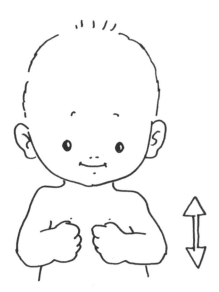

BATH

Rub body with fists.

Sign Language for Babies and Toddlers

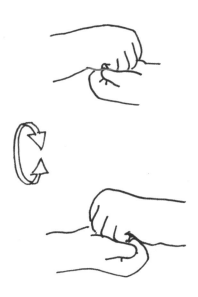

CHANGE

Hold fists together, then switch positions.

QUIET

Put index finger to lips.

Sign Language for Babies and Toddlers

TOOTHBRUSH

Rub R index finger across mouth.

DARK

Palms in, tips up, move down while crossing in front of eyes.

6. Feelings

This is an important section, as it represents the expression of things that could cause pain and discomfort to a child and which he may be unable to express. Many of the things contained within this list will often cause a young child to throw a tantrum and become upset, so it is of the greatest benefit to everyone if some of these needs and emotions can be communicated.

LIKE

Place R index finger and thumb on chest, close together while moving away from body.

SORRY

Circle "S" hand clockwise on chest.

COLD/FLU

Grasp nose with thumb and index finger of R hand, then move away, as if using a handkerchief.

CRY

Place index fingers under eyes, slide fingers down cheeks,
showing where tears would flow.

SICK

Tap forehead with middle finger of modified "8" hand.

LAUGH

Place index fingers of both hands on sides of mouth and
flick out two or three times.

SMILE

Place index fingers of both hands on sides of mouth and move up to cheeks.

SURPRISE

Place both index fingers and thumbs at side of head.
Snap open into "L" hands.

AFRAID

R and L "5" hands, palms in, tips facing. Move up and down
several times as if shaking with fear.

COLD

R and L "S" hands, knuckles facing. Bring hands close to body and pretend to shiver.

FUNNY

Brush tip of nose twice with tips of R "U" hand.

HAPPY

R hand against chest, palm in, tips left. Brush up chest twice.

SAD

Both palms against cheeks, move down face.

ANGRY

R claw hand at chest, palm in, move up and to the side.

GOOD

Touch lips with fingers of R hand, move forward
into upturned L palm.

LOVE

Cross hands over heart.

DRY

Move R "X" hand from L to R across chin.

FINE

R "5" hand, palm L, place thumb on chest and move slightly forward.

HUNGRY

Draw tips of R "C" hand down the upper chest.

Sign Language for Babies and Toddlers

NICE

Place R palm on top of L palm. Slide R hand away from L.

TIRED

R and L bent "5" hands, palms in, place tips on chest. Turn hands
downward, ending with little fingers on chest.

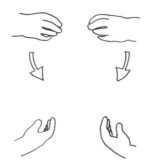

SOFT

Palms in, open and close thumb and forefingers of both hands.

7.   Other Useful Words

These are signs that, despite being useful and relevant, cannot be categorized in any of the preceding sections. You will doubtless have your own words to add to this list and the other lists within this chapter.

HI

Wave hand.

WHAT?

Brush R index finger across open L fingers.

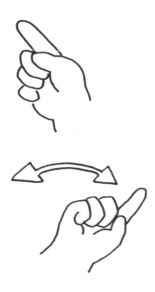

WHERE?

Wave R index finger from L to R, palm out.

WHO?

Move R index finger clockwise around mouth.

WITH

L and R "A" hands, touch knuckles together.

AGAIN

L palm up, fingertips out, arc R bent "5" hand to L palm and touch with fingers.

THERE

Point R index finger out at location.

ACCIDENT

R and L "S" hands, knuckles facing, strike together.

Sign Language for Babies and Toddlers

EAR

Pinch R earlobe with R thumb and index finger.

FACE

Circle face with index finger.

HAT

Pat top of head.

NECK

Tap neck with R hand, palm down.

LEG

Pat R thigh with R hand.

DROP

Hold R "S" hand at shoulder level, palm down, and open fingers
as if dropping something.

LIGHT

"O" hand above head, palm down. Open fingers into "5" hand.

MIRROR

R "5" hand, palm in front of face, twist slightly to R and repeat.

TELEPHONE

R "Y" hand, place thumb on ear and little finger on mouth.

TOILET

Shake R "T" hand from R to L several times.

GIVE

R and L "O" hands, palms up. Move forward while opening fingers.

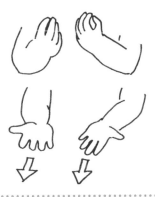

KNOW

R hand palm in, tips up. Tap forehead.

TAKE

R "5" hand, palm down. Draw up quickly, ending in "S" hand.

DOWN

Point index finger down.

COAT

R and L "A" hands, palms out. Move hands in,
as if pulling coat to body.

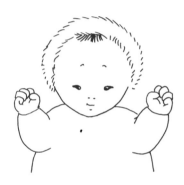

CAR

R and L "S" hands, mime steering.

- -

DIRTY

R hand under chin, palm down, wiggle fingers.

HAIR

Rub hair between fingers.

SMALL

Palms facing, tips out. Draw close together.

OUT

R bent "5" hand, fingertips in L "C" hand, both palms in.
Draw R hand out, ending in flat "O" hand.

UP

Point up.

WAIT

Wiggle fingers of both hands, L hand forward.

SHOES

R and L "S" hands, palms down, knuckles out, strike together twice.

....

RAIN

Both hands above head, palms down. Bring down while wiggling fingers.

SIGN

Move index fingers in alternating circles.

SIT DOWN

Lower hands with palms down.

STOP

One palm up, quickly tap with edge of other palm.

WALK

Palms down, alternate placing one in front of the other to mime walking.

UNDER

Move R "A" hand under L hand, palm down.

WIND

Move R and L "5" hands from side to side.

PACIFIER

Suck on finger and thumb.

BUS

R and L "B" hands, R little finger against L index finger.
Move L hand out and R hand in.

WATCH/CLOCK

Tap R index finger on L wrist.

GO

Point fingers in direction you are going.

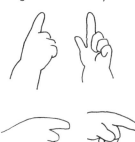

CLEAN

L palm up, tips out. R palm down, tips L. Brush R across L,
as if wiping clean.

DIFFERENT

Cross index fingers, palms out, move apart.

FAT

R and L bent "5" hands, bounce off cheeks.

MANY

R and L "O" hands, palms up. Open into "5" hands, palms up.

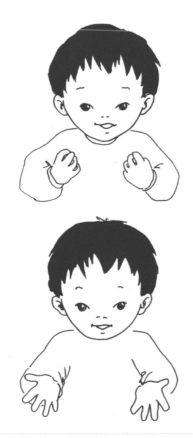

OLD

R "S" hand under chin, palm in, move down in a wavy motion.

SAME

Bring R and L index fingers together, palms down and tips out.

WET

R and L "5" hands, place R index tip on the mouth, then drop both hands into "O" hands.

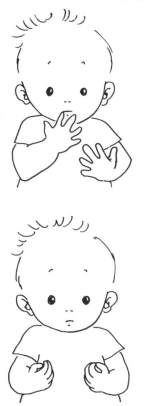

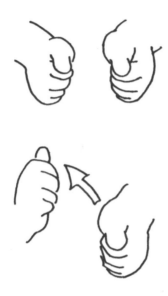

BEHIND

R and L "A" hands, knuckles facing, thumbs up. Place hands together and draw R hand back.

IN

Place fingertips of R bent "5" hand into L "C" hand.

Forming Simple Phrases

We have discussed the obvious advantages of using American Sign Language vocabulary wherever possible. However, at this stage, for the uninitiated, it is important to explain that when forming simple phrases in sign language, although the ASL vocabulary is used, it is far more common for the phrases to be loosely structured in the format used in Signed English. American Sign Language was based on what Thomas Hopkins Gallaudet learned in France, which is why its formal grammatical structure is loosely based upon that of spoken French. An easy example is that adjectives are often used after nouns, such as "The balloon red," "The man tall," and "The woman old."

Although it is a tremendous advantage for a hearing child to have knowledge of sign language, this cannot be to the detriment of his learning spoken English in the correct grammatical form. The same thing applies to a deaf child, of course. When he starts to learn to sign, it is important that he learns to sign using the word order that is commonly used in spoken English (ensuring that the lip pattern he is observing and the word being signed represent the same word at the same time), hence the development of Signed English. To summarize, American Sign Language provides the vocabulary of signs that are used, while Signed English uses that vocabulary in the word order that is familiar to us in spoken English. Signed English is easily understood by all hearing-impaired people who use sign language. American Sign Language, however, is often the language of choice of many deaf people. By using the grammatical structure of ASL, a deaf person is able to communicate more quickly and abbreviate certain facets of the spoken language. This also enables a sign-language interpreter to translate simultaneously in the public forum, whereas if Signed English were used, it would require a great deal more time for the translation to be completed, making it far less efficient.

Once your child has shown his basic grasp of a few signs and, to your delight, joy, and amusement, is using them frequently and correctly, you have a sound basis to begin linking some of these words together to form simple phrases. Again, do not be discouraged should you observe that a phrase is being used incorrectly—all you need is another dose of the patience and gentle encouragement that you used with your child when initially learning your first few words together.

Just as time and experience will have meant that you have been able to make the transition from just signing one word at a time, you are now progressing to the stage where you can successfully communicate using simple phrases. As with all learning, this needs to be a gentle but steady learning process. Phrases need to be two or three words initially, but as you progress, this can be built upon. Of course, a young child will not want to communicate using phrases of seven or eight words, since he has simple needs that only require simple communication. However, as your mutual signing skills develop, you may decide that the time has come to begin using signs as you learn nursery rhymes or simple songs together. This is the natural progression from the very simple phrases contained in this chapter.

Once your child has mastered some of the two-word combinations, he or she will be one step further along the path to becoming a more accomplished communicator. Although we have noted that every child progresses at his or her own pace, it is common for this to be achieved between the ages of sixteen and twenty months. There's no need to be alarmed, though, if this should happen either sooner or later. The next step is to express entire ideas. To get you started, there are a few examples of longer phrases at the end of this section.

MOMMY SMILE

MY BROTHER

MY FRIEND

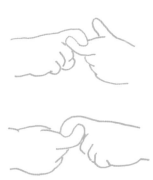

DADDY FUNNY

GO BED

LOVE MOMMY

ARE YOU THIRSTY?

WOULD YOU LIKE MILK?

PLAY WITH THE BALL.

WHAT'S THAT NOISE? LISTEN.

From Sign to Speech

You are now at the stage where you have successfully mastered some sign language skills with your child, and you should always be simultaneously speaking the word, phrase, or sentence that you wish to communicate.

A deaf or hearing-impaired child may utter sounds, but being unable to hear the spoken word, the sounds made will not be those that emulate normal speech. As she is unable to hear the spoken word, she will have no basis on which to copy it. If you have already raised a child and not used any sign language, you will be quite familiar with the way that gurgles and squeaks develop through the stage of sounds that are almost recognizable as words into simple words that we can understand. The words will not always be correct, but the basis of verbal communication has been established and the learning process has started.

Just as there is never a specific time for every child to begin learning to sign, similarly there is no right time to shift the focus of communication from sign language to speech. However, this process will actually be dictated by your child's need to stay in almost constant communication with you. One of the strongest natural impulses in a child is that of curiosity. This natural curiosity will eventually be the catalyst for speech to become more significant than sign language in your child's understanding of what is going on around her.

In your interactions with your child using sign language, you need to be constantly within her line of vision in order for the communication to be successful. However, daily life is not like that in reality. Once she has a basic understanding of speech, which has been significantly helped along the way by the use of signs from an early age, your child will realize that suddenly there is speech going on around her and that she is able to understand this speech despite the fact that she is not receiving signs simultaneously. This may well be because she is not directly involved in the conversation. However, being curious by nature, once this communication channel has opened, she will want to be able to participate.

When you realize from your child's reactions that she does understand speech (you can test this easily by asking her, using speech only, if she would like some ice cream, a cookie, or whatever her favorite treat happens to be), then you can begin to actively encourage the use of more speech. However, do not tell her not to sign, since sign language will continue to be of use in a variety of circumstances. The way to progress to this stage is to simply speak to her from farther away and from places where you cannot easily be seen. Of course, not being able to see you clearly, she will not know if you are signing while you speak. If you place your child in (safe) situations where she needs to communicate with you but cannot see you, again, you will encourage her to use the voice that she has recently discovered. For example, if she is in her high chair in the dining room, you call out from the kitchen, "Tell Mommy if you'd like some ice cream." She may well sign as she speaks, but you are encouraging the speech process.

Having acquired some knowledge of sign language, it is important not to suddenly stop using it, since there are many occasions when it will be of use. The most important is being able to communicate with deaf and hearing-impaired people. Sign language is still a major part of their lives, and it is important for as many hearing people as possible to be able to communicate with them in their own language, making integration as complete as possible.

How many times have we developed a secret language or code to be used with a friend when we want to communicate something in a public situation that for various reasons we do not wish the entire assembled group to understand?

This is another good example of when sign language can be useful. However, an example in terms of a child is when he needs to use the bathroom urgently, but it is something that the child and his parents do not wish anyone else to know. Similarly, in a public situation, a parent may wish to reprimand a child for perhaps being too noisy, but without the embarrassment of having to make a public spectacle of what is going on. Sign language can also be used in a noisy situation or, assuming visual contact is possible, when one is too far away from someone for speech to be heard. For example, sign language is used by many scuba divers.

Interestingly, a further progression using sign language as a communication aid should be mentioned. I recently conducted a small experiment using sign language. When trying to teach a five-year-old native German speaker to speak English, I employed the use of sign language, at the same time teaching another child of the same age without the use of signs. The difference was amazing in terms of how quickly the child taught with both sign and speech learned the new English words, compared to the child who was taught just using the spoken word. The learning process is made easier in two separate ways when sign language is employed. The obvious way is that so many of the signs offer an obvious visual clue that make understanding a great deal easier. When trying to learn two things simultaneously, one thing supports the other—the two actions enable the brain to comprehend more easily, almost making the learning process twice as efficient.

Having taken the time to read through this book and possibly to put into practice some of the suggestions that have been made, you should have every success in your attempt to offer your child the advantages of learning sign language at an early stage in his development.

Your Questions Answered

Having considered many of the questions asked by parents who have attended talks about introducing signs to babies or who have read other articles about the subject, we hope that these frequently raised points may answer some of the most important questions you may have after having read this book.

Q. You have said that parents need to be observant, as sometimes the signs are given so fast that they can almost be missed. Why, then, does it take my child so long to respond to a question?

A. Yes, it is quite true that once they have realized what they want to express, babies will often sign very quickly. However, they are at a very important developmental stage; their thought processes are developing and growing just as their bodies are. Once a baby has realized something that he wishes to express, then you can easily miss what he is trying to tell you. For example, just after a meal, your little one may be sitting in his high chair, decide that he is thirsty, and suddenly sign "Want drink!" You have not asked the question, so you have not provoked a response. In other words, you have no idea how long it has taken him to think about his thirst and ask you for a drink. While the signs can be delivered quickly, the thought process is not necessarily a quick one and you will need to be patient when you have asked questions. You can almost see the thought process working, but it can take quite some time for the question to be considered and the answer formed. However, once the answer has been decided you will see it is usually given with great enthusiasm. You will also come to realize that as the baby grows and the thought processes develop, the time between a question being asked and the answer being given will gradually shorten.

Q. Although we are eager to use sign language, do you think it can give any clues as to how much comprehension has really taken place in terms of a child's awareness and understanding of what is going on around him?

A. Child psychologists have often blamed certain types of behavior on things that happened at a very young age, frequently before the person concerned has any conscious childhood memory. We are convinced that the use of sign language has opened an entirely new area of proof that we do comprehend a great deal at a very early age, even if this does not become part of our conscious memory. Having understood what happened, even if we were unable to express our thoughts about it, these events may easily remain in our unconscious mind and influence what happens in the future. To cite an example, a mother tells us the story that as part of her conversation with her son, one of the usual questions asked during their morning sign session is, "Where is Daddy?" Previously, he had always used the reply "work"—this is what he had learned as the response to the question and was always his father's true location. However, on this particular morning, instead of giving his usual "work" response, he made the sign for an aircraft. He had remembered that the previous afternoon he had been in the car when his mother drove to the airport, where his father was dropped off to fly out on a business trip. This example proves that both true comprehension and memory are present at an early age.

Q. Although we are interested in using sign language with our baby, we both have busy professional lives and just can't find the time to introduce it into our routine. Do you have any suggestions as to how we can do this?

A. Yes, there is an increasing use of sign language at the preschool level, and we would encourage you to find a preschool where sign language is used. If you establish a good relationship with your preschool, they can actually be the people who are doing the teaching of the new signs, with you providing the backup and practice at home. We do understand that circumstances can dictate certain time restrictions; however, there is no reason why you cannot employ sign language inventively during the time you do have together.

Q. We are using sign language at home but do need to use a preschool for a few hours each week. Although there are excellent local facilities, sign language is not used at them. For a part-time preschool situation, would you consider it worth going to a place farther away, or is our child getting enough exposure to sign language at home?

A. Of course, the more practice and exposure your child has, the better, although we take your point that it is only a few hours each week. Assuming that all the sign language learning is done at home, there is another advantage of your using the preschool where sign language is used. Apart from learning to communicate with other family members, it is a great opportunity for your child to be in a situation with others of the same age and be able to communicate with them. You would be amazed at how quickly preverbal children who use sign language communicate with each other and, most importantly, learn to share. They can be observed asking each other for toys, and the preschool staff encourages them to sign "please" and "thank you" when they give and take. Learning to share is an important lesson, both with other children and siblings at home, and using sign language helps teach this lesson early.

Q. Understanding that it is important to sign as often as possible, when do you think my child will be the most responsive?

A. Basically, as with all learning, we are much better when our minds are alert and fresh, so the morning is a good time. Naturally, we all need to tend to our comforts before we are able to concentrate, so we would say that your very best time is when your child is still in his or her high chair right after breakfast. However, remember that you can be signing constantly and use sign language during breakfast, offering choices and allowing your child to sign his or her response. After breakfast, however, new learning can begin.

Q. We are eager to use sign language, but our child seems to lose interest and diverts his attention to other things. What can we do?

A. For a baby to learn anything, he needs to be enjoying himself and you need to keep his interest. If you find his attention is wandering, then it is up to you to come up with other ways of keeping his attention. Next time you are doing some signing with him, observe his reactions. Obviously, just as there are times when his attention wanders, so there are other times when he laughs and appears to really be enjoying the activity. What are you doing when he is thoroughly enjoying himself and engrossed in what you are doing? Whatever that happens to be is something that interests him, so do it more often. You need to repeat that particular activity frequently, but whatever the activity is, keep the format but change the content on a regular basis to keep the activity fresh and interesting. Don't forget that you are the "performer" trying to attract your audience—your own "performance" needs to be as animated as possible, so your best pantomime acting is a must!

Q. I understand the importance of repetition, but won't my daughter start to become bored doing the same thing over and over again?

A. Not if you are inventive yourself. The repetition we are referring to does mean using the same word, but constantly changing the context in which it is used. Remember to keep offering choices, which can be incorporated into your teaching. Let's say it is mealtime and you are trying to introduce something new, let's say a banana in this instance. Let's also assume that you have already taught her to sign and understand "apple" and "orange." Previously, you have offered a choice between those two familiar fruits. Having introduced the banana, you ask if she would prefer an orange or a banana. The next day, the choice offered would be between the apple and the banana. By looking through a storybook, you will easily find an illustration of a monkey eating a banana. In another session, ask questions about the picture: "Is the monkey eating an apple or a banana?" While it is imperative to repeat the sign of the new word and constantly practice it, you can easily alleviate boredom by using it in a variety of situations in this way, always asking questions but offering a choice of answers.

Index

Acknowledgments

Thank you to Mrs. Vasti Stols, Qualified Early Years and Special Needs teacher and baby signing specialist, who advised on the Question and Answer chapter.

Picture credits: © Digital Vision 7, 8, 9, 10, 13, 15, 16, 17, 18.

Illustrations by Anne-Marie Sonneveld. http://web.pncl.co.uk/~anne-marie/